Doing Your Part

Together We Can: Pandemic

By Shannon Stocker

21st Century
Junior Library

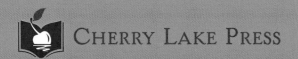
CHERRY LAKE PRESS

Published in the United States of America by Cherry Lake Publishing Group
Ann Arbor, Michigan
www.cherrylakepublishing.com

Reading Adviser: Marla Conn, MS, Ed., Literacy specialist, Read-Ability, Inc.

Photo Credits: © RW Jemmett/Shutterstock.com, cover, 1; © Daisy Daisy/Shutterstock.com, 4; © Pra Chid/
Shutterstock.com, 6; © Rose Makin/Shutterstock.com, 8; © Rick Menapace/Shutterstock.com, 10; ©
Stock-Asso/Shutterstock.com, 12; © Layne V. Naylor/Shutterstock.com, 14; © fizkes/Shutterstock.com,
16; © Yavdat/Shutterstock.com, 18; © FERNANDO MACIAS ROMO/Shutterstock.com, 20

Library of Congress Cataloging-in-Publication Data

Names: Stocker, Shannon, author.
Title: Doing your part / Shannon Stocker.
Description: Ann Arbor, Michigan : Cherry Lake Publishing, [2021] | Series: Together we can: pandemic |
    Includes index. | Audience: Grades 2-3 | Summary: "The COVID-19 pandemic introduced many changes into
    children's lives. Doing Your Part looks at the ways we can all mitigate risk and work together. The book gives
    actionable suggestions to help young readers be active in overcoming obstacles as we navigate the current
    outbreak. These books include science content, based on current CDC recommendations, as well as social
    emotional content to help with personal wellness and development of empathy. All books in the 21st Century
    Junior Library encourage readers to think critically and creatively, and use their problem-solving skills. Book
    includes table of contents, sidebars, glossary, index, and author biography"—Provided by publisher.
Identifiers: LCCN 2020039967 (print) | LCCN 2020039968 (ebook) | ISBN 9781534180086 (hardcover) |
    ISBN 9781534181793 (paperback) | ISBN 9781534181090 (pdf) | ISBN 9781534182806 (ebook)
Subjects: LCSH: COVID-19 (Disease)—Social aspects—Juvenile literature. | Epidemics—Social aspects—Juvenile
    literature.
Classification: LCC RA644.C67 S744 2021 (print) | LCC RA644.C67 (ebook) | DDC 362.1962/414—dc23
LC record available at https://lccn.loc.gov/2020039967
LC ebook record available at https://lccn.loc.gov/2020039968

Cherry Lake Publishing Group would like to acknowledge the work of the Partnership for 21st Century
Learning, a Network of Battelle for Kids. Please visit http://www.battelleforkids.org/networks/p21 for more
information.

Printed in the United States of America
Corporate Graphics

CONTENTS

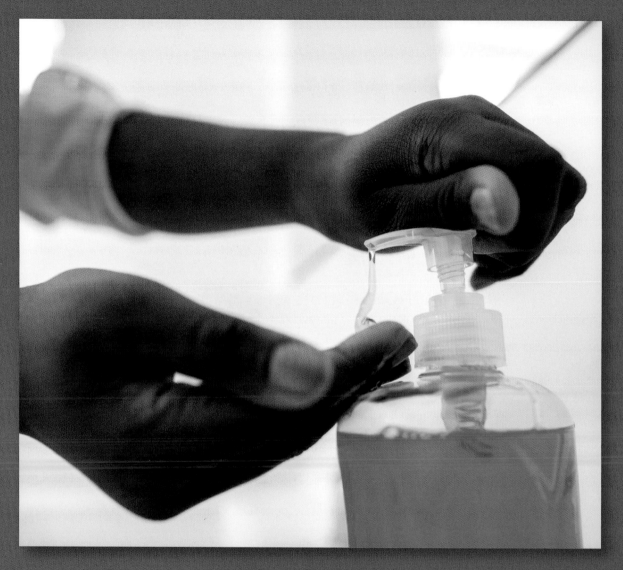

You should wash your hands for as long as it takes to sing the ABC song!

Making a Difference at Home

If everyone in the world gave you a penny, do you know how much money you'd have? Over seven BILLION dollars! That's a lot of money! Think about it. To get that much money, everyone only had to help a teeny tiny bit.

The same is true during tough times, like the **coronavirus pandemic**. Making a difference doesn't take a lot of effort. And you certainly don't have to be an adult! But it does take **initiative** and **cooperation**.

Some people are sick and don't even know it!
Wearing a mask protects others around you.

Everyone gets frustrated and sad sometimes when they're stuck in **quarantine**. It's hard to stay happy all the time when we can't see friends and family. One of the easiest ways to help spread joy is to reach out through technology or phone calls. Maybe your grandparents are lonely. What about a friend who has no siblings? Staying in touch is a great way to lift loved ones' spirits.

Think!

What's your talent? How can you use that to make a difference?

Even if you feel comfortable getting close, remember that someone else may not. Stay 6 feet (2 meters) away to do your part.

Pandemics can make people fearful that they'll be stuck inside for a long time. When this happens, they sometimes **hoard** supplies. People might stock up on things like toilet paper, cleaning supplies, and masks. This can cause a shortage that leaves others in the community without anything at all. You can do your part by using less at home! For example, one squirt of soap is enough to wash your hands thoroughly. If you use less, you can buy less. Then there's more to go around in the community!

Make a sign for your yard or window to show your thanks.

Making a Difference in the Community

How do you feel when someone tells you that you've done a good job? It probably makes you feel warm and happy inside. The same is true for our **essential workers**, like delivery people, doctors and nurses, and grocery store workers. During a pandemic, they're risking their lives to help keep this world running. Greeting them with smiles and a thank-you is an easy way to do your part.

What could you send to Love for Our Elders?

Did you know that small acts of kindness can help someone feel loved, even if they don't know you? Nursing homes are filled with older people who are alone during quarantine. But you can make a difference with a piece of paper and crayons! Write them a letter. Tell them a joke, discuss your favorite hobbies, or draw a picture! An organization called Love for Our Elders will send your handwritten letter to someone in need. Your small **gesture** will bring that person a huge smile.

Look!

Who are the essential workers in your community?

Sidewalk chalk drawings are a great way to spread sunshine!

All across the country, people are decorating their windows to bring a smile to those walking by. Hearts and rainbows have become **symbols** of hope, happiness, and good things to come. Many communities have even turned the activity into scavenger hunts!

Create!

Start a scavenger hunt in your neighborhood! Ask neighbors to hide a rainbow in one of their windows. See how many you and your friends can find.

Unless your parents are actually teachers, this is new for them too.

Making a Difference at School

Schools all over the world had to close because of the coronavirus. So how can you do your part when you're learning from home? The easiest thing to do is to keep a positive attitude and help your parents help you! You can help by reading instructions before asking for help, picking up after yourself, and being patient with your new "teachers."

Donating unused clothes or toys is a great way to help.

Many families could use some help getting books to their homes. But thanks to organizations like First Book, almost 2 million books have reached children through emergency feeding sites and homeless shelters. So how can you help? Brainstorm ways to fundraise with your family and friends. Maybe you could host a used book sale or throw a virtual read-a-thon. Use the money raised to make a donation to First Book!

Create!

Send a homemade card to your schoolteachers to show that you miss them.

Help friends celebrate big days with car parades.

As you can see, making a difference doesn't have to involve hours of hard work. It doesn't have to be expensive. It means doing the things you love to make other people happy. It means doing the things you can to keep your community healthy. It means being considerate, thoughtful, and kind.

Doing your part is fun!

GLOSSARY

cooperation (koh-ah-puh-RAY-shuhn) the act of working together to achieve a common goal

coronavirus (kuh-ROH-nuh-vye-ruhs) a family of viruses that cause a variety of illnesses in people and other mammals

essential workers (ih-SEN-shuhl WUR-kurz) people who provide work that's necessary to keep a community safe and healthy

gesture (JES-chur) an action that expresses good intentions

hoard (HORD) to collect a large supply of something, often hiding it away

initiative (ih-NISH-uh-tiv) the power to take charge before others

pandemic (pan-DEM-ik) an outbreak of a disease that affects a large part of the population

quarantine (KWOR-uhn-teen) the state of being isolated from others

symbols (SIM-buhlz) marks, designs, or characters that represent something else

FIND OUT MORE

WEBSITES

Feeding America—Find Your Local Food Bank
https://www.feedingamerica.org/find-your-local-foodbank

First Book—8 Million Books
https://firstbook.org

Love for Our Elders
https://loveforourelders.org

INDEX

ABOUT THE AUTHOR

Shannon Stocker writes picture books, books for young readers, and *Chicken Soup* stories. She enjoys watching her children do their part by writing letters to people, helping around the house, and thanking essential workers daily. Shannon lives in Louisville, Kentucky, with Greg, Cassidy, Tye, and far too many critters.